MANY OF THESE SONGS APPEAR ON:

Jeff Mell!n Saves the World, Parts 1ne & 2we
Good for a Gander
The Eddies Come Apart & Other Minor Diasters
   Best Recordings: 1993-1997
Skin & Bones

ALSO BY JEFF MELLIN

99: A Novel in Numbers

OTHER KOLOURMEIM TITLES:

Garrett Caples
   Synth
   The Philistine's Guide to Hip Hop

Willam Diaper
   Nereides: or Sea-Eclogues

John Hoffman
   Chapbook (The Hermetic Edition)

Christopher Nealon
   Ecstacy Shield (Black Square Editions)

S&B

SKIN & BONES

SONG LYRICS BY JEFF MELLIN

KOLOURMEIM PRESS
TRADE-MARK
OAKLAND, CA

These lyrics are administered by Sweet Red Onion Publishing (BMI) and are reprinted here with permission.

Photographs © 2004 John Soares (www.johnsoares.com)

"Pop on the Easel: The Art of Jeff Mellin"
© 2006 Garrett Caples (www.garrettcaples.com)
Originally published in *Rock Heals: A Narrow House Weekly*

Book design ©2008 Jeff Mellin, Big Blue Ox (www.bigblueox.net)
Typset in Chyelovek and Warnick Professional

Special thanks to the Harvard Museum of Natural History
(www.hmnh.harvard.edu)

Published by Kolourmeim Press (www.kolourmeim.com)
P.O. Box 1514, Oakland CA 94604
in partnership with
STEREORRIFIC Stereorrific Recordings (www.stereorrific.com)
and Big Blue Ox (www.bigblueox.net)

FIRST EDITION (PAPERBACK)

ISBN 978-0-6151-8126-4

Printed in the United States of America

"And I could say Oo oo oo
As if everybody knows
What I'm talking about
As if everybody here would know
Exactly what I was talking about"

— Paul Simon

for Yvonne, Oo oo oo

CONTENTS

'VE OFTEN THOUGHT THAT READING SONG
lyrics as poetry can be like walking up a broken
escalator. Even if you can, it's a little awkward,
and you miss out on a pretty essential element of
the experience.

Still, I've spent plenty of time poring over the
tiny text on album liners, cassette inserts and CD
booklets trying to fully absorb what my favorite
singer-songwriters and bands were actually sing-
ing. Occasionally I've found the truth disappoint-
ing — to this day, I can't believe that Morrisey
didn't go "to London and die."

Usually, though, the liners reveal something
new, give me a better sense of the song craft, sto-
ry and message, and, ultimately, a more complete
appreciation of the song as a whole — even for
songs I didn't like. With that in mind, I humbly
present this collection of some of my own lyrics.

MY FIRST INSTINCT HAD BEEN TO PRESENT
the songs in the order they had been written, but
as the songs settled into place, I found the order

based more on when I had recorded or released the songs — even just as home demos — felt more natural and relevant. So, some of the songs in the last chapter are actually quite old, but, for whatever reason, took years to take form and "fit" with whatever else I was doing.

That said, the first chapter is mainly a sampling of my early, earnest, coffeehouse stuff. The second covers some of the better lyrics written for my old Boston pop group, the Eddies*, as well as some written when I should've guessed the Eddies would soon be breaking up.

The next chapter begins with "Frankly, Babe," the first song I'd written after I had accepted that fact. It's a fairly straightforward, tongue in cheek pop song, but I still think of it as the boat that took me across that river. The rest of that chapter covers the songs that became *Saves the World, Parts 1ne & 2we*, as well as some I'd recorded around that time to pitch to other artists.

The final chapter begins with songs for *Good for a Gander* (some of which never made it onto the record) up through the best of what I've written

---

*Apparently, some band in California is calling themselves "the Eddies" these days. Perhaps they're named after my old band? I suppose it's not worth arguing with them about it at this point, but I feel like I ought to at least point it out. Don't be fooled! Only genuine 1990s Boston-based Eddies music will satisfy!

since leaving Boston for Virginia and now Phila-
delphia (not including the *Sticky Fingers Suite*, for
which I'm afraid you'll just have to wait).

Before you dig in, I should point out that
my beautiful gal, Yvonne McCarey (who's got more
of a natural artist's sense than she let's on), handed
me the title and refrain for "Where You Goin' With
That Bag O' Nuthin' For No Good Reason?"; that
the chords and melody for "Blue Corduroy" (sadly,
inaudible here) were co-authored by my old band-
mate, Jake Guralnick; and that I stole the opening
line of "Come Apart" verbatim from something
Garrett Caples said after an all-night road trip.

I should also mention that the cover and
chapter photographs were taken by John Soares
in the singular Museum of Comparative Zoology
at Harvard University. Founded in 1859 through
the efforts of Swiss born zoologist Louis Agas-
siz (1807-1873), it's one of the hidden gems of
the Boston area. Some of my fondest childhood
memories include coming in with my dad to
get lost in its maze of glass and wood, skin and
bones. The displays are dated, the cases crowded,
but as you stand eyeball to glass-eyeball with the
whole of natural history you can't help but feel
at once transcendentally connected and mortally
awestruck. They don't make museums like it any-
more. There's talk now of moving the collection

to a more modern facility, so I'm really glad John was able to take these photos while its strange nineteenth century charm is still intact.

John and Garrett have each been a huge influence on me as an artist, and I'm honored by their contributions to this book. I'm also indebted to idea machine Jeff Maisey for putting this book idea in my head (whether he knows it or not); to my brother Joel Mellin and everyone else who has believed in these songs enough to help perform and record them with me over the years; to everyone in the "Den" who challenged me to write better way back when; to my Papa and Uncle Peter for teaching me how to play in the first place; to Mom and Dad for their encouragement and for instilling in me an appreciation of words and music (and having such a great folk music LP collection); and especially to Yvonne, for a million reasons — like, for instance, putting up with all of this nonsense.

I DOUBT ANY OF THIS WILL BE CONFUSED WITH "literature," but I do hope that, as a companion to my recordings, it can provide the sort of insight and (more likely) disappointment I was always digging for in those cassette liners. Plus, once you stop laughing, you'll be able to sing along.

Jeff Mellin
Philadelphia

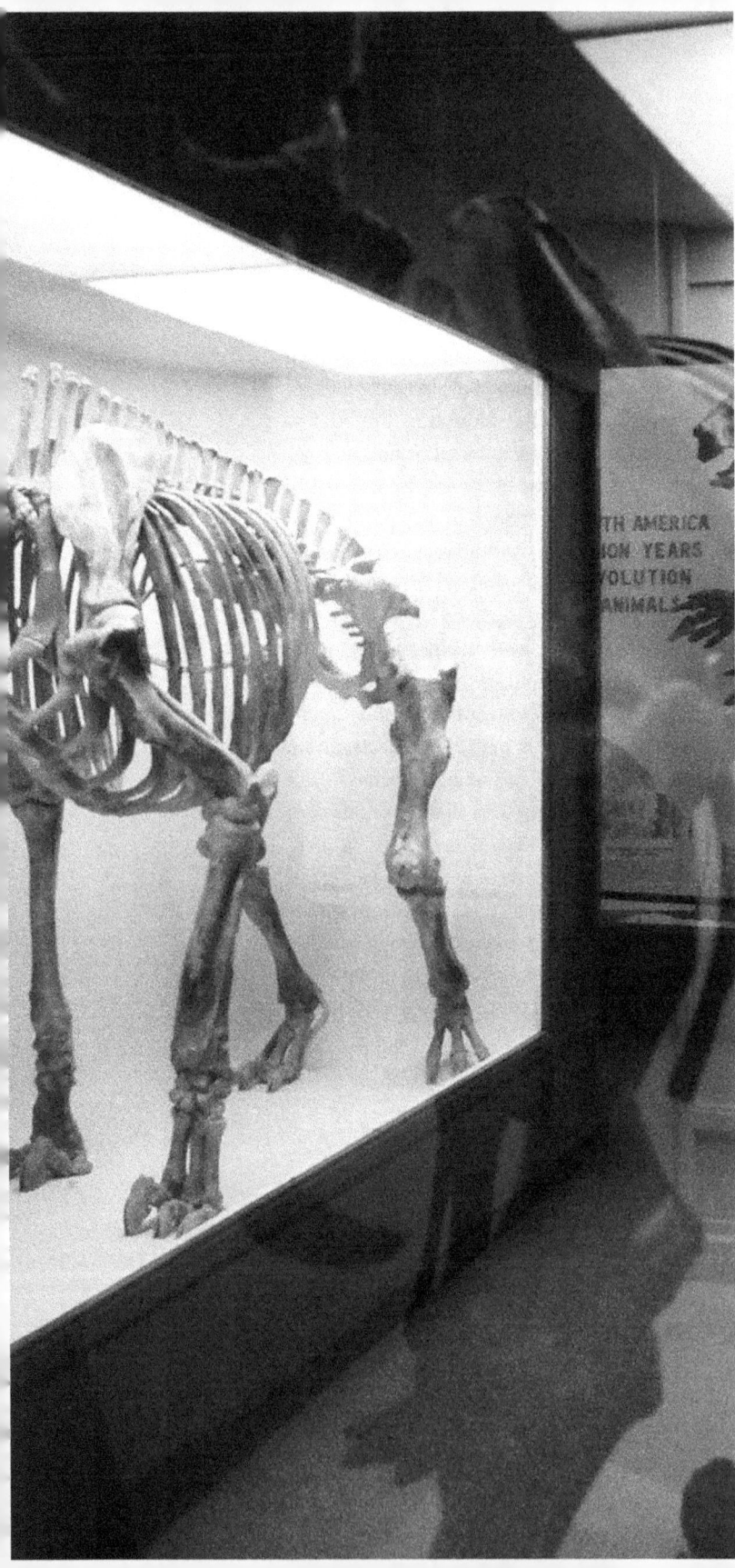

POP ON THE EASEL:
THE ART OF JEFF MELLIN

J EFF MELLIN WAS THE FIRST AND QUITE possibly only genuine pop song writer I've ever met, despite the fact, years after our initial encounter at Livingston College (Rutgers University), I've unexpectedly become an occasional, half-willing, professional music journalist. What I mean is that Jeff was the first person I met who approached both the art and the craft of the pop song from a perspective close to my own as a listener. He had an enthusiastic yet by no means uncritical appreciation of the classics (the Beatles, say, or Dylan) but too could savor those genuine, if ephemeral or even vapid pleasures, of Brill Building hackery, Tom Waitsian Cole Porterism, Jim Croce's AM radio tongue in cheek, Donovan's "I Love My Shirt." The joy of pop songs is often quite simply their utter ridiculousness, for which Jeff retains a keen, though unironic relish. Some of my favorite memories of college are just sitting around his dorm room, paging through the massive hardbound Beatles studio session logbook, seeing who added what little part when, wanting to know how it was done in the studio, though, as a songwriter armed solely with an acoustic guitar and Johnny Cash's pickless style of strumming, Jeff had already arrived. He wrote crazy good songs like "Geologic Time," a genre-piece of the you-don't-like-me-so-I'm-leaving-not-that-you-give-a-shit-anyway school, which climaxed with the embittered long view of: *you think you are so pretty, think you look so fine, but girl your life won't mean a thing in Geologic Time*, a conceit which allowed him to work in words like "trilobites," which is what seems to me the true goal of pop lyricism.

Later after college, when he began making music in studios, his writing changed, with perhaps slightly less emphasis on the obvious lyrical cleverness necessary to the naked acoustic strummer, just as Dylan's going electric afforded him a whole new set of writing possibilities. Yet still Jeff would endlessly turn out gorgeous lines like *she reads my face like a novel, but she skips to the end of the book*, or brilliant changes in scope, like *a frog on the back of a whale*, both from "Typical Male," a song he recorded with his mid-'90s pop garage band, the Eddies. And of course his art continues to evolve in unanticipated directions, like the golly-Buddy-Holly

simplicity of "Blue Corduroy," from his 2001 solo album *Good for a Gander*.

Still, while it's often difficult to gauge the worth of pop lyrics printed on the page without musical accompaniment, it's remarkable how well this book of lyrics reads, as lyrics in the poetic sense. Slightly archaic, perhaps, with their unfussy rhymes, though entirely free of neoconservative Wilburism in the handling of line and meter, Jeff's lyrics considered as poetry at their best evoke the only-just stylistically-belated (late 1940s), yet entirely individual and intense poems of Weldon Kees; even at their least effective, they have the readable lightness of Edward Arlington Robinson, and everyone knows Paul Simon made "Richard Corey" into a better song than it ever was a poem, which illustrates my point nicely.

Being a close friend and collaborator, my feelings on Jeff's abilities are perhaps biased. All I care to add is the fact that Jeff once took a poem I wrote, "Light Sleeper (Elegy for George Harrison)," and turned it into the lyrics of a beautiful tribute to one of the most profound men ever to have the mantle of "pop star" thrust upon him. (Coincidentally, I'd copped the title "Light Sleeper" from a song, by Oakland rapper Saafir, the Saucy Nomad.) Clearly Jeff and I were both feeling Harrison's loss in a similar way, though

I was astonished he wanted to use my poem instead of his own lyrics, which are so goddamn good. It may be the highest complement my poetry has ever received.

Garrett Caples
poet and critic
Oakland

1 JUST PROP ME UP...

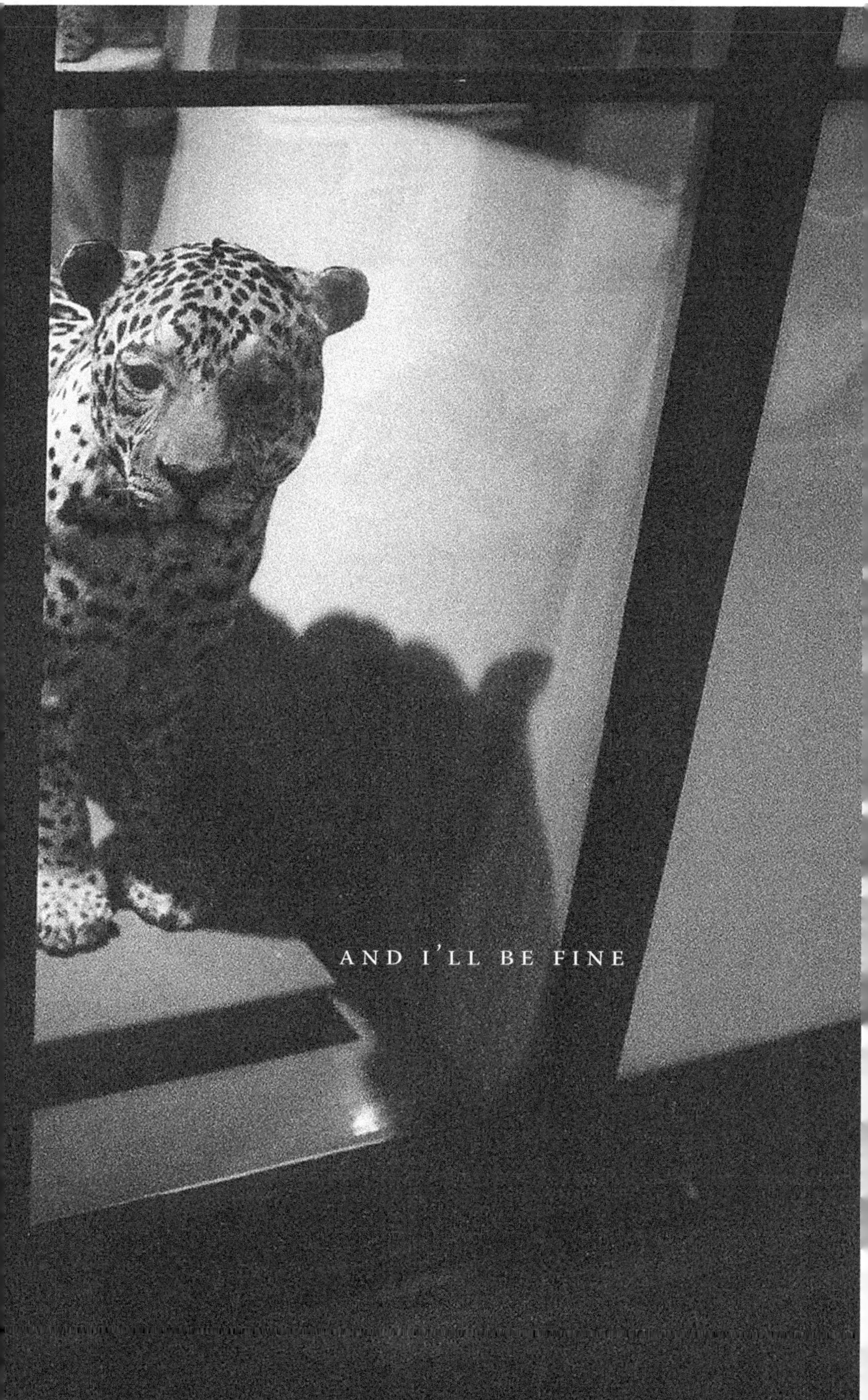

AND I'LL BE FINE

Paper Door

Knew a girl who had an attic apartment
with a paper door
She'd sit on her second-hand carpet
and read magazines on the floor

Disguised in the dark of the room,
the window shades pulled down
And she'd say, "Why should I be on display
for this backwards little town?"

People often asked her
why she didn't mind the view
She said, "I have grown accustomed to myself,
why haven't you?
I have grown accustomed to myself,
why haven't you?"

Boy in the room downstairs
hunts his pockets for laundry change
Pulls out a picture of someone
he'd lost in a verbal exchange

He sits in the dark of the room
like she sits in the dark of his heart
And he says, "I gotta get out of this place
and get myself a new start."

People often asked him
where it was he planned to go
He said, "When I become accustomed to myself,
I'll let you know.
When I become accustomed to myself,
I'll let you know."

Girl in the attic apartment, she fell asleep
Lost in her second-rate articles
Lost in her paper beliefs.

Boy in the room downstairs holds a picture
He holds it hard
The only thing keeping him here
is the one thing he can't discard

Nighttime dulls the anger
and the morning comes too soon
Daylight grows accustomed
to the darkness of the room
Oh! The morning always comes to soon

Ballad For My Great-grandfather

Now, I was told this as a boy
I don't know if it's true
A story of Great-grandfather
who sailed the ocean blue

He said, "I have just turned twenty.
I'll soon be twenty-one.
Stockholm I must leave behind
before the setting sun,
       before the setting sun."

He signed aboard a clipper ship
before the sun went down
The ship was called the *Anna Lee*
and bound for Boston-town

His empty heart filled like the sails
aboard the *Anna Lee*
and though the sea was all around
he knew that he was free
       he knew that he was free

Now when he got to Boston-town
he met a lady fair
with eyes are blue as oceans and
with sea-mist in her hair

Great-grandfather, he married her
for she had won his heart
and when the light of morning came
they watched his ship depart
        they watched his ship depart

So he became a blacksmith proud
He worked the metal and the tin
but ironworks and metal bars
can hold a free man in

Great-grandmother,
she kept the family
or at least she tried
Half the time she raised the children
Half the time she cried
        Half the time she cried

One night he'd had to too much to drink
A pistol in his hand
It's sad to see a sailor sink
when dry upon the land

He said, "Darling wife, I love you,
but is this all I can be?"
Great-grandmother, she wrapped her arms
around him like the sea
        around him like the sea

Now I have just turned twenty-one
I'll soon be twenty-two
and my life lies before me like
the mighty ocean blue

Oh, Great-grandfather, I know that you
have left it all to me
and I will do my best for you
as I set out to sea
as I set out to sea

SALAD DAYS OF CLEOPATRA

In the salad days of Cleopatra
lingering at Quannapowitt Lake
in the back of Tony's car
lavished in security and kisses on the neck
she let Tony hold her tightly in his arms

He said, "Rome may into Tiber melt!"
She opened like the Nile Delta
Tony filled her body like a well
He took her home as morning fell

A river flows
A well runs dry
Another day
and I'll get by

Afternoons alone now, Cleopatra
dreams of Egypt by the river
dreams of kingdoms by the shore
watching the activities of people in the street
from a room above a Hallmark store

She gave birth to a little child
Egypt melted in the Nile
They got by on the little Tony made
She closed her eyes and there she stayed

A river flows
A well runs dry
Another day
and I'll get by

Every year it was the same —
Cleopatra took what came
and as it came it fled
Years go by without retreat
Swelling hands and swelling feet
Cleopatra sinks into her nursing bed

And she says, "Once upon a time
I was the queen of the civilized world
I was the queen of my home
And I have seen a century go by in an afternoon
And I have seen my children grown

My daughter took me in her car
and said, "I'm gonna take you far away —
Gonna take you someplace new."
She stuck me here
What am I supposed to do?

A river flows
A well runs dry
Another day
and I'll get by

🯁

JUST AFTER

May 25th
Track 11
My lover's arrival is scheduled for 5:00
A blackbird takes off from a telephone wire
It breaks the monotony
Wakes up the sky
The red in its wings
strikes a chord in the sunlight
and then it is gone
like a song that escapes into midnight

Summer drones on
like a fever
We stare into space without saying a word
Grounded in silence
Perhaps I should leave her, I think
but the red of her lips reassures
Now, Mars is red
but Venus is there in the morning
and a blackbird will catch your attention
and fly without warning

Long-distance call
on a Sunday
We walk on a wire
with passion and stealth

I cross the line
at just the wrong time
and get snagged in the snare
I have set for myself

Now, losing my mind
over her would be absurd
but her lips are as red
as the red on the wing
of a blackbird
Her lips are as red
as the red on the wing
of a blackbird

THE EARTH IS ROUND
(THE EARTH IS FLAT)

My confidence was buried in my head
like a stone
like a stone worn smooth
      by the rush of a river
and it's sinking slowly down into the bed
as the water rushes over me
      with everything you said

Water's rolling down my cheek
Kiss me soft
Kiss me sweet
Yeah, I know —
We've been through that
The Earth is round
The Earth is flat

Your sympathy was falling from your lips
like the Earth
like the Earth as it falls
      one more time around the sun
and as the sun was rising you woke to find instead
of a feather in your cap you had
      a wrinkle in your bed

Feather drifts
down to my feet
Kiss me soft
Kiss me sweet
Yeah, I know —
We've been through that
The Earth is round
The Earth is flat

I watched a promise buried in the earth
like a stone
like a stone that breaks
        with a change in the weather
The stone was heavy
The earth was cold
but your head at my breast
is as light as a feather
Your head at my breast is as light
as a feather

BREAKDOWN IN CAMBRIDGE

Stuck in the traffic on Commonwealth Avenue
and the city's slow and old
Yeah, the city's slow and old
Over the river and then I'll be free of you
and the bridge groans with the cold,
Yeah, the bridge groans with cold

And the light shifts from green into red
I remember when you said,
"This is my favorite view of the city.
The place where the sky leans down
          to meet the Charles."
You leaned into me like the sky into water
and the light of the moon was as soft
as the night in your arms

And I heard you talking in your sleep
about the things you've got on your mind
I wonder if we'll keep anything from this time

Breakdown in Cambridge is tying up everything
and I think you're gonna call
I still think you're gonna call
I ignored everything you tried to say to me
like the cat trapped in the wall
like the cat trapped in the wall
And the light shifts from red into green

I'm rewriting the scene where you say,
"Won't you please stay here tonight in the city.
From the roof of my brownstone,
            we'll watch the moon fall in the Charles."
I looked at you,
but you looked to the water
and the look in your eye was as clear
as a fire alarm

And I heard you talking in your sleep
about the things you've got on your mind
I wonder if we'll keep anything from this time

Found one of your cigarettes under the front seat
and the car still smells like smoke
Yeah, the car still smells like smoke
It's soaked in my skin
and my clothes
and upholstery
like the butt end of a joke
like the butt end of a joke

And the light's just as yellow and grey
I can still hear you say,
"You wouldn't love me if I weren't pretty."
and "October's as brown as the moon
            in the mud of the Charles."
The moonlight came down
like a fist through a mirror,

14

and the look in your eye cut as deep
as the glass in my arm

And I heard you talking in your sleep
about the things you've got on your mind
I wonder if we'll keep anything from this

SOLID GROUND

Wrinkled suit and borrowed tie
Around my neck like a long goodbye
We hung around, 'till it got late
You couldn't stand the extra weight

How far did you drive before you got here —
leaving behind everything you've been given?
Now you've arrived, you've made it so clear
You've driven too far
to end up back in New England

The radio said rain was due
You said, "The radio sounds just like you."
But static blocked the full report
Static laughs at me for sport

How far did you drive before you got here —
leaving behind everything you've been given?
Now you've arrived, you've made it so clear
You've driven too far
to end up back in New England

Suit me up and spit me shined
Just prop me up and I'll be fine – I'll be *fine*
I couldn't think 'till you came 'round
You can't think on solid ground

The rain came down, and there it stopped
I saw you'd gone when I got up
But nothing's changed – I still can't think
The dishes pile up in the sink

How far did you drive before you got here —
Leaving behind everything you've been given?
Now you've arrived, you've made it so clear
You've driven too far
to end up back in New England
Driven too far
to end up back in New England

2 WROTE DOWN MY MISTAKES

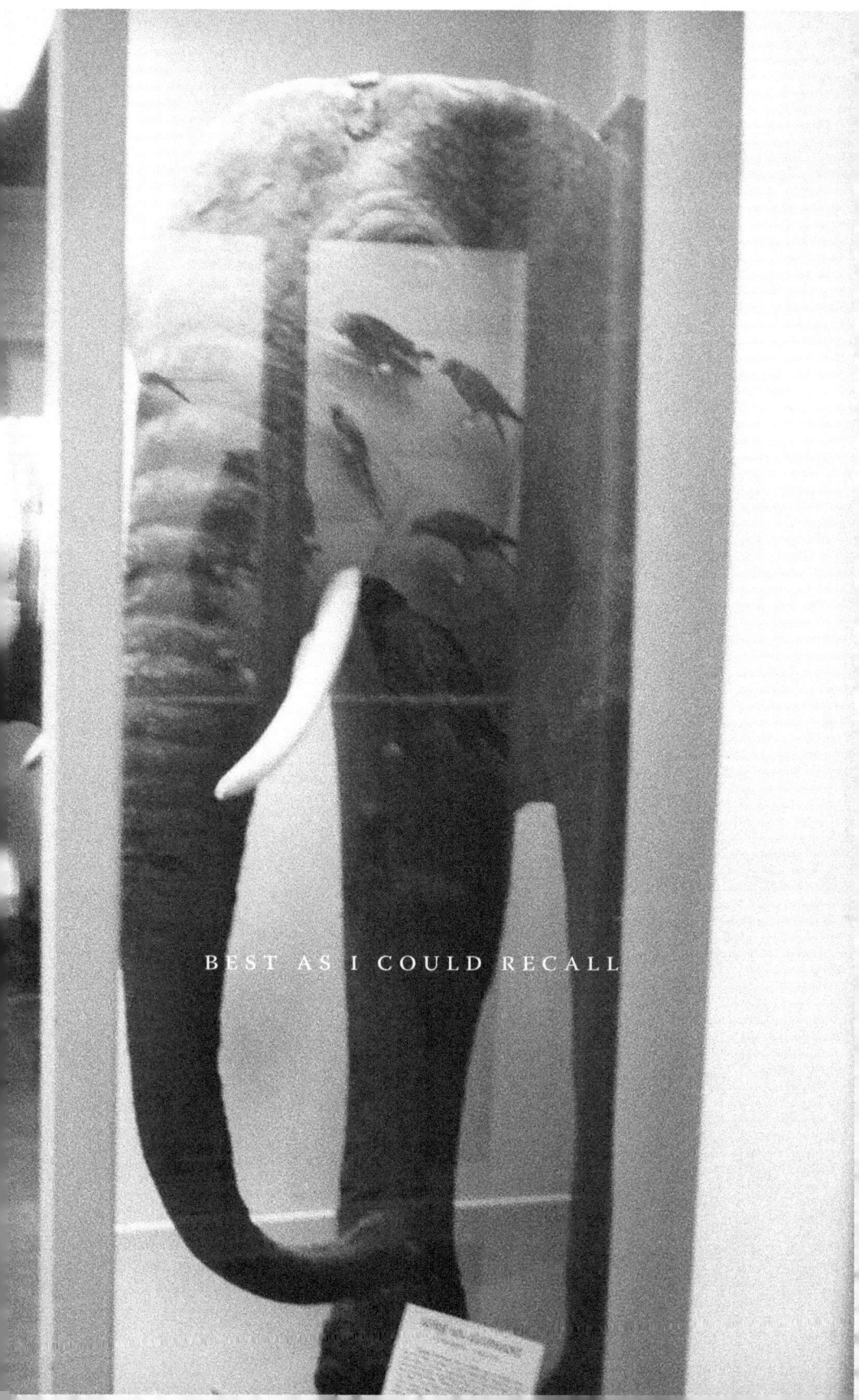
BEST AS I COULD RECALL

COME APART

I've been up for days because I couldn't sleep
I've come unglued
I've come unglued
Midnight in the kitchen in my stocking feet
The soles worn through
The soles worn through

Should've known
about this from the start
That we'd come apart
We'd come apart
We'd come apart
We'd come apart
One more
overturned applecart
As we come apart
We come apart
We come apart
We come apart

I wrote down my mistakes best as I could recall
You were the least
You were the least
I read them over once, then I made paper dolls
But saved your piece
I saved you're piece

Should've known
this all would go to waste
That we'd come apart
We'd come apart
We'd come apart
We'd come apart
Gave you a diamond ring
when what we need is paste
As we come apart
We come apart
We come apart
We come apart

I've been up for days because I couldn't sleep
I've come unglued
I've come unglued

LONDON BRIDGE

Following the sun on the horizon
Following your fingers through your hair
You were following the life you'd had your eyes on
while I'm here falling down a flight of stairs
with London Bridge
on my back
I've been picking up the pieces
Picking up the slack

As I lay at the base
you said you needed more space
You wrinkled your brow,
your ambivalent face
like Marie Antoinette
with a lit cigarette
Now my head's in your lap
like a debutante's pet

I walked across a bridge in Arizona
but thought that I had seen it somewhere else
I voiced my observation to the owner
who said I ought to keep that to myself
But then he smiled,
as if to cover up the cracks
while he was picking up the pieces
Picking up the slack

And you said, "That's all very nice,
but you told me that twice,"
and, "If you really cared
you'd take my advice."
                    And then it all clicked
like a match to a tick:
We were wrong from the start
We're unmatched and unfit

And I say,
"London Bridge is falling down
falling down falling down
London Bridge is falling down,
            my fair lady."

Belly-up and bleached beneath the sunshine
Pregnant with the hope of changing tide
The country dug its boot-heels in the incline
The country thought the incline would subside
Ooo, but you know better
You got no reason to look back
You'd just be picking up the pieces
Picking up the slack

London Bridge is falling down
falling down falling down
London Bridge is falling down
my fair lady

Typical Male

She holds her tongue like a switchblade
I hold my tongue in my cheek
She's thin as a passing example
but her girth will inherit the meek

She says her mood's always changing
I say, "I'll hang on
like a frog
on the back of a whale."
She replies,
"Do you think that you're helping at all?
You typical, typical male."

She reads my face like a novel
but she skips to the end of the book
She binds me with doubts and assumptions
but I'm bound to stick 'round for the hook

I say, "Now, this can't be right,
'cause I had it all planned
Right down to the final detail."
She replies, "You think skies
can be framed by a window,
You typical, typical male."

Downtown selecting our groceries
The closest we'll get to an aisle
I wouldn't say we're in agreement
but I guess it'll do for awhile
I guess it'll do for awhile
I guess it'll do
for awhile

GIVE AN INCH

You were on my mind
and I'm here thinking everything
is working out fine
But you had other plans
The words you're using now with me
are cold as you're hands

If you want perfection
you had better get a ruler
'cause if I give one more inch
you'll find the measurement peculiar

You wrote me from Detroit
You dodged the situation
with your words, so adroit
Your letter was in verse
The mood was antiseptic
but the meter was worse

If you want consistency
you're better off with pudding
'cause if I give one more inch
I will surely lose my footing

So, now you're far away
and I'm here trying to think
of something clever to say
The envelope's addressed
My handwriting's legible
but the letter's a mess

I could make excuses
for my immature behavior
but there's nothing I could tell you
that would ever win your favor

You were on my mind
You were on my mind
You were on my mind

Forever, Anne (a Date)

Burned my hand on the stove again
and the smoke and the burn that resulted in turn
only fanned the flames
I know I could bite back now
like a dog bites his mange
She was out of my reach
Now I've found that she's out of my range

It's my own fault, I do suspect
I held her kisses and purrs like and entrepeneur
holds the stub of a check
Oh, I told her I loved her
I told her I cared
She just totaled my weaknesses
Tolled me for all the repairs

Dry as a soda cracker
Why won't she call me back?
I know that it isn't too late
Clock ticks
My patience's taxed
Now, why won't she call me back?
Don't wanna be waiting here
forever, Anne
forever, Anne
forever, Anne

(a date)

Lately, it's been a sorry, sorry scene
I've been leaving my house
just so I can go back
and check my answering machine
Yeah, my heart's in the right place
but there's a part that I lack
See, my design would be fine
if I just had a spine in my back

Dry as a soda cracker
Why won't she call me back?
I hope that it isn't too late
Clock ticks
My patience's taxed
Now, why won't she call me back?
I know I'll be waiting here
forever, Anne
forever, Anne
forever, Anne

(a date)

TURN FOR THE WORSE

Back
of a taxicab
built for two
The vinyl
and the silt
The residue of guilt
spilt between a phone call
and her bluejeans
               So it seems
She's taken a turn for the worse
Taken a turn for the worse
Making a sow's ear from a silk purse

Stink
of the Lincoln Tunnel
shows no mercy
Plaster and rust
are cast away like trust
and thrust upon the bosom
of New Jersey
          Mercy, mercy!
She's taken a turn for the worse
Taken a turn for the worse
Making a sow's ear
from a silk purse

But me,
I'm taking my time
Taking my time
'till I can get where
I can take a turn for the better

                            Have you seen the
Hudson River late at night?
           The stars line up upon the Tapanzee
               like Christmas lights

And have you seen the stars upon
           the Hudson River after lunch?
The stars line up
      like teeth
      in my glass jaw
      awaiting your next punch

And have you seen the way he looks at you
           with starry starry eyes?
He wants to tell you he could love you
But he's too afraid to try

Taking a turn for the worse
Taking a turn for the worse
Making a sow's ear
from a silk purse

SMILE LIKE A LEMON PEEL,
KISS LIKE A PAPER CUT

Turn out the lights—
        What's that she's concealing?
High as a kite
up all night
painting patterns on the ceiling?

And I'm sprawled out on the hardwood,
begging her pardon
best as I could
Paint hits the ceiling fan propeller—
spits and sprays
She'll be cleaning up the mess she's made for days

Smile like a lemon peel
Kiss like a paper cut
        How does she make you feel?
        How does she keep it up?
Salt in the burn from a cigarette butt
Smile like a lemon peel
Kiss like a paper cut

Bait her with oranges—
        her eyes will do the chewing
like a forlorn syringe
that might have been a greater man's undoing

Her apartment floor was slanted. Still,
I couldn't understand how
every suggestion
I had planted rolled beneath her bed
Guess they're safer there
than stranded in her empty head

Smile like a lemon peel
Kiss like a paper cut
> *How does she make you feel?*
> *How does she keep it up?*
Salt in the burn from a cigarette butt
Smile like a lemon peel
Kiss like a paper cut

With her hair tied up in ribbons
a pie in the face could be forgiven
I'm licking my lips for every trace
but something stays
We'll be cleaning up the mess we've made for days

Smile like a lemon peel
Smile like a lemon peel
Smile like a lemon peel

WISHFUL THINKING THINKING

It went off like a rocket
in the palm of my hand
You were calm, in command
I was done and damned

When the cops tried to stop it
they were unprepared
but you weren't scared
'cause you're the one who'd put it there

And every time
somebody brings it up
it brings me down
it brings me down
I wish I knew what you'd wanted me to be
Now it's wishful thinking
thinking you'd wish you were here with me

It went off like a pipe-bomb
in your pocketbook
You were shocked and shook
from the blow you'd took

When I tried to defuse it
you'd sat by nonplused
sipping orange juice
like a broker of abuse

And every time
somebody brings it up
it brings me down
it brings me down
I wish I knew
what you'd wanted me to be
Now it's wishful thinking
thinking you'd wish you were here with me

BLUE EYES /
BRIGHTON BUS STOP

Blue eyes saw the danger,
but I didn't even flinch
That night I was so green
you must've thought I'd be a cinch
You say now I'm too starry-eyed
to waste your precious time
but that's OK —
        I know my vision's fine

Blue eyes raw with anger —
You just blamed it on my youth
And packed me in you suitcase
with your socks and shopworn truths
You say we'll meet again —
You'll just be back to pick my bones
But that's OK —
        I'm better in my own

No I won't cry —
The possibilities are open as the sky

Blue in all directions
Flawless as a child at birth
The eggshell of the planet
The eyelid of the Earth

You left me like a cloud
that breaks up into atmosphere
But that's OK,
       'cause now my view is clear
That's OK —
       Now my view is clear

3 YOU'VE BORNE THIS

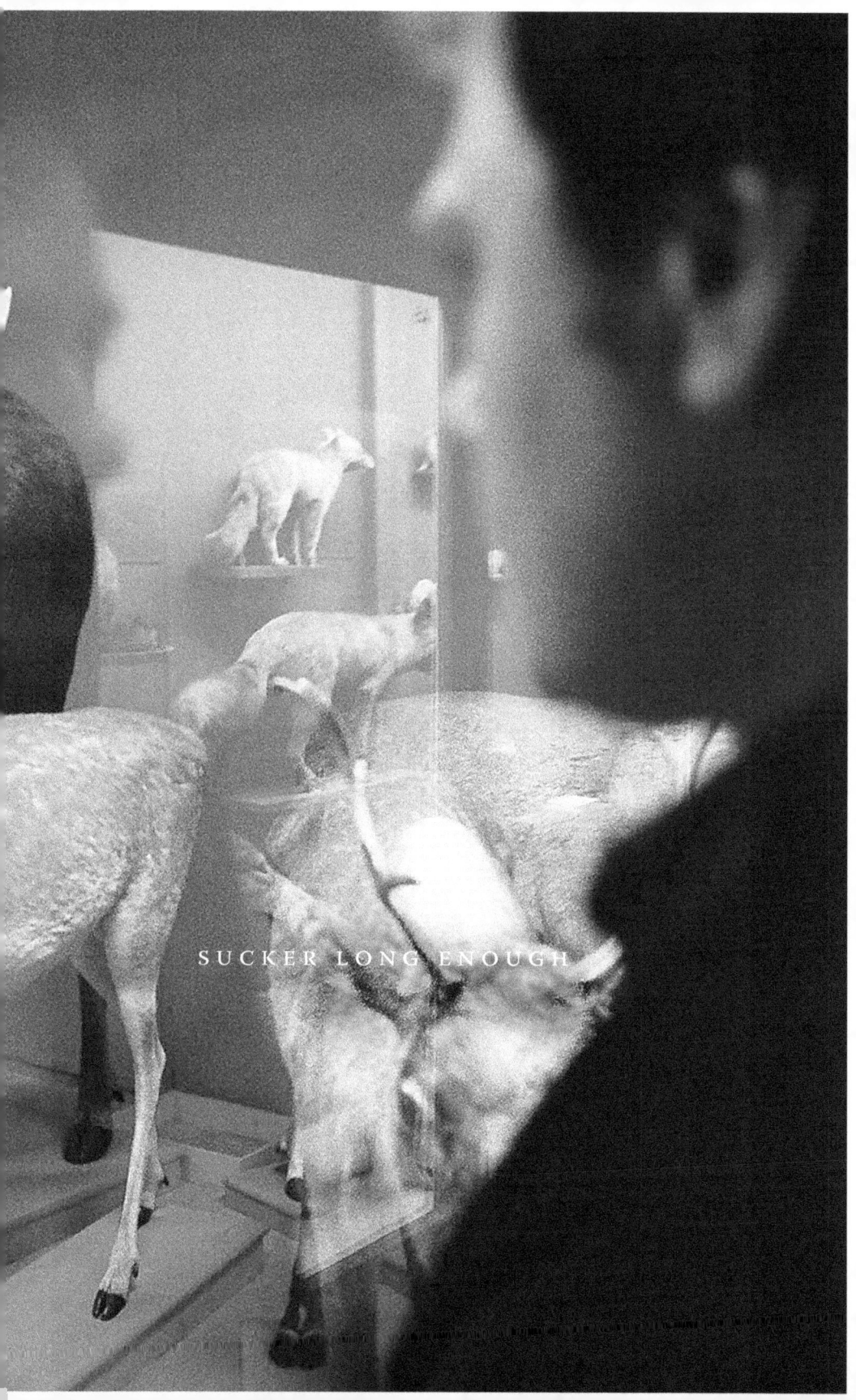

SUCKER LONG ENOUGH

FRANKLY, BABE

When
I was twenty
I thought
I had plenty to spare
I was sharp
I was bright
I could stay up all night if
I dared

Now
I'm confused
I've been bull–whipped
and bruised
I pull out
what is left of my hair

You don't care

Just for a minute
I thought
I could grin it and bear
Face the occasion
with calm
grace
and smooth debonair

Now
to refute
check the back of my suit—
There's a boot
where there should be
a chair

You don't care

I know
I've failed again—
I'm immersed in despair
Trails
I've traversed
left me worse
for the wear

When I woke up this morning
the sun wasn't there

You don't care

LEVER BIG ENOUGH
TO MOVE THE WORLD

See her pretty face
Her waiting eyes
To face a girl like that
I'd need the strength
of twenty men my size—
skin and bones
skinny ties

I've got a lever big enough
to move the world, oh can't you see?
Where can I find a love
that's big enough
for just one girl and me?
Just one girl

I'm off kilter
I'm off balance
like a clown
I built a pedestal for her—
How will I ever get her down
to console me
to confound?

42

SHOCKED (AT FIRST)

Sure it hurts, but
I figured it would work this way
Up your shirt were
dirty tricks that you had yet to play
like debts unpaid
and lies you'd yet to lay
Hey, hey
Hey, hey

And the band played "Isn't It Romantic?"
You cocked your head
like the *Titanic*
just to let me know
you'd sunk so low
I was shocked (at first)
but understand that I can let it go

Sure it hurts, but
don't wait for me to die of grief
What's the moral?
Bore a hole
below a coral reef
to find beneath
your quarrel's got no teeth
Tee–hee–hee
Tee–hee–hee

And the branding iron's in the fireplace
so strike your mark upon my pretty face
and watch it glow,
then sign below
I was shocked (at first)
but understand that I can let it go

You hung in your chair
'till you almost fell backwards
Your black hair
brushed the floor
as those four words came out so slow
and stole the show
I was shocked (at first)
but understand that I can let it go

Where You Goin'
with that Bag o' Nuthin'
for No Good Reason?

She got a bag full o' nuthin'
for no good reason—
A tag on her muffin, but I know she's teasin',
'cause she showed up just as I was
easin' into that style —
cowboy hair an' a country mile
'lectric record players on the checker'd tile
singin', "Yeah, yeah, yeah! Alright!"

She kept her flag half–masted
just to draw attention
to the trust–fund punks
an' the lust–drunk pensioners
When I showed up
you coulda cut the tension with my guile—
sidelong muttonchops an' pickerel style
stickin' country music records
in the punk–rock pile
singin', "Yeah, yeah, yeah! Alright!"

She says, "You look like a million people,
You look like a million people
You look like a million people...
Man, I've seen enough of that!"

WILSON SQUARED
AIRPORT DISASTER

A good cry'll drive it out of you
like rain'll drive an earthworm from the ground
I'll pick up
      where I left off —
             go down to Wilson Square

    so I can stand around

            What's it gonna take
            What's it gonna take
            What's it gonna take
            for me to break through?
            Oh! For me to break through

          ...and the attendant
       from the duty–free shop
hands me a handkerchief
as I watch you walk
through the airport gate in disbelief
He says, "This time it's no fake.
You can tell 'cause she didn't look back."
Still, I drop my 'kerchief
      like a referee
           at the half

What's it gonna take
            What's it gonna take
            What's it gonna take
            for me to break through?
            For me to break through

Oh! For me to break!

Half–Moon in 4/4

Half–moon
Half–moon
Could go either way
Half–moon
Half–moon
Could go either way
They say it's getting darker—
They can't see the darkness for the grey

I sipped my wine
She slipped in
like a sugarcube
I sipped my wine
She slipped in
like a sugarcube
I said, "If you're so sweet, Babe,
how could you be so rude?"

Half–moon
Half–moon
Could go either way
Half–moon
Half–moon
Could go either way
They say it's getting darker—
They just can't see the sunshine for the day

She took off her head—
the American girls always do
She took off her head—
the American girls always do
I cleared a space on the table
to provide her with a better view

Half–moon
Half–moon
Could go either way
Half–moon
Half–moon
Could go either way
They say it's getting darker—
But, you can't believe a thing they say

She lay down her arms,
but I didn't have the stomach yet
She lay down her arms,
but I didn't have the stomach yet
Well, I knew what was coming
but wondered how much more I'd get
get
get

Half–moon
Half–moon
Could go either way

She stepped up her feet
as she whispered
that at least she'd tried
She stepped up her feet
and she whispered
that at least she'd tried
Her seat was empty
but the table was piled high
                     high
                     high

Half–moon
Half–moon
Could go either way
Half–moon
Half–moon
Could go either way
They say it's getting darker
but it looks like she's gonna stay

LAST STRAW

Between the Devil and the ocean
he draws a cigarette from the pack
He thinks with one last Camel
he can fake a lack of emotion
He was cold as the ocean
He was slow as Manassas in '62
The troops wore camel coats, worn right though
the civil talk all afternoon

Eyebrows raised like a court reporter's
amazed a razor stays upon its track
He knows his memory is short
but the straw he's drawn is shorter
He was cold as a razor
He was bold, he was clever and never fooled
Lever pulled when he swore knew
when to stop, when to let it stew

Memory and ocean air
against a sea of seashell soldiers
standing shoulder bare to shoulder
I swear it all came down to splitting trigger hairs
I swear... he was cold on the trigger—
He could hold on forever or see it though
but bit by bit there was more to chew
'till he lost the war and caught the flu

OH-NO, JOEY TUSSAUD

When I grow up I'll be a wax man
glass–eyed and taciturn
in my wax suit
Lost
and exhausted
in nights of wax fruit
like this—
something like this...

Look at these hands—
they weren't made for these tools
correcting complexions
on paraffin fools
Where is my courage
to knock out their stools
like this?
Something like...

So, lately I'm planning a trip to the sun
If the spaceship don't melt
then it's easily done
The wax moon is waning
but I've just begun,
like this—
something like...

RIGHT ON!!

Get out of your skin,
and put the record right on
    Right on
        Right on
            Right on
Get out of your skin,
and put the record right on
    Right on
        Right on
            Right on

You say you're bored
before you even begin
Why don't you wipe that face
from your stupid grin
and write on?

Step out of your mind
and take a look at yourself
Step out of your mind
and take a look at yourself

You want the world
It won't cooperate
So you're acting like the people
that you used to hate

You lost your soul
        —at least you've still got your health!

Take off your shoes
and take a look at your socks
Black and blue
—you gotta take one off

You gained perspective
You gained control
You gained the world
but you lost your rock and roll
Lost your rock and roll
Lost your rock and roll

JUST WANT TO
SEE YOU TONIGHT

I don't know what to say, girl
How to make this alright
I don't know what to say, girl
I just want to see you tonight
I just want to see you tonight

Bust from within me
like a crowbar
bent on spite
Headstrong
and musclebound
and teeth clenched for a fight
Just for a minute
you were far and
out of sight
Just for a minute
I was drowned

I don't know what to say, girl
How to make this alright
I don't know what to say, girl
I just want to see you tonight
I just want to see you tonight

Deaf from the pressure
The measured ridicule

55

Just an observer
at the bottom
of the pool
I led you down here—
Now I wait
and hope
that you'll wrap your arms around me
like a life–preserver

I don't know what to say, girl
How to make this alright
I don't know what to say, girl
I just want to see you tonight
I just want to see you tonight
I just want to see you tonight

HAPPY FOR YOU

Just my luck
I didn't play the part
I thought the invitation read, *"Come as you are."*
But lately, I just haven't felt the same
and all you seem
to care about
is your good name

I started thinking maybe that
I'd wear your your garden party hat
and act like all the people who
were happy for you

Just my luck
It's up to me again
to do what I've been told
or lose a longtime friend
But though I know
you'd never turn away
lately I just can't believe
the things I hear you say

I grit my teeth
I thought I should
split my feet from where I stood
and like the wood beneath a screw
be happy for you

Just my luck
you're letting me down here
You've borne this sucker long enough
You've made that clear
But burrowed in that furrowed brow you've got
more than you had asked for
like or like it not

I could've gave you more I guess
and saved away that shabby dress—
the bitter sis' of Mister Blue
Happy for you
Happy for you
Happy for you

Farewell, Belle Starr

The teller turned quick
but he never got far
My lead check in his neck and his head
and I signed it "Belle Starr"
Well, I get what I want
and I want all I can
A girl wants to be wanted —
I'm wanted from here to Cheyenne
Ah-ee, hee-ee-AH-ee
Oh, from here to Cheyenne

One day by the river
on a horse black as coal
rode a man dressed in black
from his hat to his back to his soul
His face was as red
as the clay at my feet
He said, "Sister, you listen to me,
And your fortune you'll meet.
Ah-ee, hee-ee-AH-ee
Oh, your fortune you'll meet."

He said, "Over that hill
comes a traveler, I'm told,
with bags full of silver
to last 'till you're silver and old."
So when he was gone

I went over that hill
and waited 'till night
when the whole territory lie still
Ah-ee, hee-ee-AH-ee
Oh, all Oklahoma lie still

Then it happened so quick
that the details ain't clear:
I jumped out of the stick
Stuck my gun in the traveler's ear
But the moonlight shone down
and I froze like a stone
for the one at the end of my gun
was a son of my own
Ah-ee, hee-ee-AH-ee
Oh, a son of my own

I suppose I should tell you
If you haven't guessed yet:
A lead ball from the gun of my son
Was the fortune I met
So I'll die in this red clay
Like a fly in jar
Write "farewell" in the clay of the river
And sign it "Belle Starr"
Ah-ee, hee-ee-AH-ee
Oh, sign it "Belle Starr"

4 LOOK ACROSS IT

LIKE THE OCEAN

YOU, SWEET YOU

Youth
sweet youth
left me
in my prime
    I'm fine
        I'm fine
Truth be told
that scene among the young
was gettin' old
    I'm fine
        I'm fine

'cause you
sweet you
you always did me right
    Outasight!
        Outasight!
Did you know?
I've been afraid to say it
So here it goes:
    Be mine
        Be mine
    Oh, please be mine
        Oh, please be mine
        Oh,
        please be mine

OH, POSSUM!

You got the look
that's gonna turn heads
that's gonna burn beds and bridges
And if it isn't too much
I'll use you as a crutch
Your calamine touch for the itches

You say it's over—
          over-done and over-fed
You float to the surface
playin' possum—
          playin' with my head

You were mistook
when you took what he had
with the good and the bad
and whatever
and though he'd done you no wrong
when I came along
you thought maybe that I'd do you better

You say it's over—
          over-done, over-fed
You float to the surface
playin' possum—
          playin' with my head

LAKE ERIE

Rain in your hair—
        little pearls
and all this time I'm trying to keep you dry
Why was I so sure
when it's the weather you prefer?

"Lake Erie's big"
                "It's no Superior"
Pond water licks the land—
        sticks it's green there
                      like mint jam
but you say,
           "Look across it
                like the ocean.
           Look a little further
                    if you can."

We'll be hand in hand tomorrow
when we splash down into Logan
after that pond-skip through O'Hare
Oh, my little pearl—
is that the trick?
Nothing to fix
if nothing's broken?

BLUE CORDUROY

Blue Corduroy
You're a lonely girl
I'm the only boy
you'll employ
My Blue Corduroy

I want to hold you
but I won't let go
Thought I told you
that I told you so
I told you so
Corduroy

Blue Corduroy
don't throw me aside
like a broken toy
null and void
My Blue Corduroy

You can't control me
I'm controlling you
I thought I told you
I was going to
I was going to
Corduroy
Corduroy

The laundry's folded
but the rent is due
That's why I sold out
and I'm telling you
I'm telling you
Corduroy
Corduroy
Corduroy

(You've Got) The Weight of the World (on Your Shoulders)

Your thoughts are like vapors
They're lighter than air
and transparent as papers
You're thoughts are as heavy
as the pile of papers
       you've got to get ready

You've got the weight
of the world on your shoulders
File your fate
in manila folders
You say, "Before this scene turns to black,
Could you please get this gorilla down
       off of my back?"
You've got the weight
of the world on your shoulders

Your eyes are as bright
as the lights on the Empire State at night
Your eyes are as dark
as the moon in the lagoon
at the heart of Central Park

You've got the weight
of the world on your shoulders

File your fate
in manila folders
You say, "This city wants me bad, and I'm willing,
but could you please get this gorilla down
        off of my building?"
You've got the weight
of the world on your shoulders

Now, dressed for disappointment
and nothing too remarkable
you turn your pretty eyes up to the sky
You say, "Remember when I used to wish
on anything that sparkled
'cause I figured that it wouldn't hurt to try?
I figured that it wouldn't hurt to try."

You've got the weight
of the world on your shoulders
File your fate
in manila folders
You say, "I wish they'd let me know before
        they let me in,
'cause the thrill of this gorilla's
        started wearing thin."

You've got the weight
of the world on your shoulders

NATIVE TONGUE

She was upset for a while
'till she thought the whole thing through
His love had fit her like a puppet
'till she forgot it wasn't true

She went from average to medium
beneath an avalanche of tedium
and in the afternoon she greeted him
smile blanched across her face
just in case
just in case

She knew her make-up wasn't right
She split the difference with her face
He would insist the same tonight
She'd make up ways to make him wait

She went from average to medium
beneath an avalanche of tedium
and in the afternoon she greeted him
smile blanched across her face
just in case
just in case

She was upset for a while
'till she thought it through again
and again

Written in her native tongue
he was someone she could bend
and again...

She went from average to medium
and in the afternoon she greeted him
smile blanched across her face
just in case
just in case

WATCH ME SHRINK

Watch me shrink
Watch me shrink
like a needle
in the eye
of a blink

If I close my eyes for a half a second
would you disappear?
If I close my eyes for a half a second
would you disappear?

If I close my eyes for a half a second
If I close my eyes for a half a second
If I close my eyes for a half a second
would you still be here?

Watch me shrink
Watch me shrink
like the needle
in the eye
of a blink

If you have a second, close your eyes
You can disappear
If you have a second, close your eyes
You can disappear

If you have a second, close your eyes
If you have a second, close your eyes
If you have a second, close your eyes
You can disappear

Watch me close
Watch me close
I'll be gone
in the blink
of a nose

THE WAY YOU'D LEFT IT

It's just the way you'd left it
I haven't changed a thing
It's just the way you'd left it
I haven't changed a thing

It's just the way you'd left it —
          Nothing's out of joint. Sometimes
a man'll lie down in the gap
to get across his point

The first time that you met me
I was wise beyond my years
My eyes were clear and lucid
My thoughts were true and real

The first time that you met me...
          Oh, but that was years ago, back when
you bet that I'd forget you

Look at that sky
That cotton-black cover
That sheet of smother
That seated mother beating
          down like wind and worry
Here's your hat, now
where's your hurry?

Look at that sky
                    Look at that sky
            Look at that...

It isn't that you changed me
It's more the way you left

            (It sounds strange to say that out loud)

It's the sound of my complaining
The sound of my ears draining
Years go by and still
the sound of my own voice
sounds closest

Look at that sky
                    Look at that sky
            Look at that...

ALLIGATOR SUITCASE

You want me to open up
Split down the middle like an alligator suitcase
Travel umbrella
Sample-sized toothpaste
for the crocodile teeth in your dissection tray

With a smile, you put it behind you
as far as it would go
But every porcelain tooth
that you lay in the wall of China's just
another brick through my window

Give me one reason
why we live like we do
I gave you all I've got but now
I'm givin' up
Givin' up
Givin' up on givin' in to you
Givin' up on givin' in

You say, "It ain't so tough. No, no, no...
                    Just take a bite. It's easy."
But you know that greasy kids' stuff's
too slippery to every please me

Give me one reason
why we live like we do

I gave you all I got but now
I'm givin' up
Givin' up
Givin' up on givin' in to you
Givin' up on givin' in

Yvonne, I Left The TV On

Wake up, Yvonne
I had that dream again
Standing in the kitchen
Standing on the airplane when the jets went dead
And you said,
      "The floor seemed more important then."

Wake up, Yvonne
I think there's someone at the door
Oh no, it's just the roar of engines overhead

Oo oo oo
If it weren't for you
Oo oo oo
I'd never make it through
Yvonne
Yvonne
Yvonne

Wake up, Yvonne
I think I left the TV on
It's nearly dawn
The light is thick
The air is strong
The Air Force choir is
singing that song that starts: *"O Say,*
                         can you see..."

Say,
what's the big idea?

Here's a big idea
Here's a big idea
Here's a big idea

Oo oo oo
If it weren't for you
Oo oo oo
I'd never make it through

Yvonne
Yvonne
Yvonne

DON'T GO CRAZY...
BEFORE I DO

Every time the pressure starts to pile on
I paste a smile on just to please you
Grin and bear may be a style you wear
but I don't care — It doesn't suit you

Don't go crazy putting on face that isn't yours
The one that you showed up in's more attractive
And don't go crazy running 'round
    in someone elses shoes
Don't go crazy
before I do

Are you surprised to find the camera never lies?
Let's point it in the wrong direction
From what I've seen
    your vision's never half as keen...
But we'll come clean upon reflection

Don't go crazy saying things
    you think I want to hear
I don't need a mirror
I need a window
And don't go crazy trying to let me in —
    Just let me through
Don't go crazy
before I do

Maybe if we figured out a plan
Maybe if I were a bigger man
Lately little triggers
pull their weight in handstands

What's the point of second guessing
how we ought to live?
I doubt that kind of thinking is productive
I'm lucky that I found you
Now I'm all you've got to lose
So don't go crazy
Don't go crazy
Don't go crazy
before I do

Sinker, Hook and Line

I played the part
I played the spoon
But how much art
can you blow in a balloon?
Can you shoot 'em that look
as your eyes dart around the room?

Face in the dirt —
Why should it matter?
The worst is over now
The Earth is flatter
I got an eye on the ball
Got another eye
on the batter

But I feel less than real
I had something in my core
but it ain't there no more
With open arms
every time
they pulled me in —
Sinker, hook and line

So here's a toast
to all who've suffered
You've given up the ghost
The batter's buttered

You're Rubin Kincaid
You're Ruben Studdard

And you feel less than real
You had something in your core
but it ain't there no more
With open arms
every time
they pulled you in —
Sinker, hook and line

HALF-CIRCLES

God is made of wheat
God is made of wheat
Grown in row on row
             repeat
             repeat
God is made of wheat

But ain't that incomplete?
Ain't that incomplete?
How far can my shadow
stretch beyond my feet
when the sun is high?

Now, love is made of sky
Love is made of sky
Deep and blue as far as you and I

Up on the moon
there's a sea — a sea of tranquility
Could it be,
that's the tune that keeps killing me?

But sooner or later
we're gonna fill in this crater

J EFF MELLIN GOT HIS START AS GARAGE BAND
caterwauler and suburban troubadour,
playing coffee houses, driveways, church
basements, galleries and subway stops from
Boston's North Shore to Greenwich Village.
After studying poetry, prose and politics at
Rutgers University, he returned to Boston to
front a jangle-pop band called the Eddies and
has since released a number of recordings as a
solo mod-folkie.

He's also an award-winning art director and
illustrator for national and regional publica-
tions, helped start *ArtsAround Boston* magazine
and quirky record label Stereorrific Recordings,
and most recently has co-founded Waxfruit
Arts Media, Inc., a not-for-profit organization
that will support and create projects connecting
indie music with other media arts.

He currently lives in Philadelphia with his
fiancée, Yvonne.

GARRETT CAPLES

A FREELANCE WRITER AND MUSIC CRITIC LIVING
in Oakland, CA, GARRETT CAPLES is the author of
three poetry collections, *The Garrett Caples Reader*
(Angle Press/Black Square Editions, 1999) and *er
um* (Meritage Press, 2002) and *Complications* (Mer-
itage Press, 2007) as well as *The Philistine's Guide
to Hip Hop* (Ninevolt, 2004), a collection of articles
on hip hop (with an introduction by Shock-G of
Digital Underground, no less) and *Surrealism's Bad
Rap,* (Narrow House, 2007), a spoken word CD.
He currently writes on hip hop and art for the *San
Francisco Bay Guardian* and is editing a lost manu-
script of Philip Lamantia's called *Tau* for City Lights
Books. He received a Ph.D. in English Literature
from the University of California, Berkeley, in 2003.

JOHN SOARES

BOSTON BASED PHOTOGRAPHER JOHN SOARES
has been called the "King-Daddy of Inventiveness".
He's always trying something unexpected, shooting
portraits in a bowl of milk or projecting stuff onto
other stuff or kicking tripods while the flash is going
off. And while the process is unequivocally slapstick,
the outcome is consistently raw and emotional and
always content based. He shoots for a lot of major
magazines and has won a bunch of big awards.

www.ingramcontent.com/pod-product-compliance
Lightning Source LLC
LaVergne TN
LVHW091158080426
835509LV00006B/743